For my magic charms: Noah, Milo, Zen and Lotus
and for Zen and Lotus' fairy godmothers Elena and Iris

www.theenglishschoolhouse.com

Copyright 2021 © by The English Schoolhouse

All rights reserved. This book or any portion thereof may not be reproduced or used in any manner whatsoever without the express written permission of the author except for the use of brief quotations in a book review. This is a work of fiction. Names, characters, places, and incidents are a product of the author's imagination. Any resemblance to actual persons, events, or locales is entirely coincidental.

ISBN: 978-1-955130-04-2

Godmothers are More than Just Fairies

Written by Dr. Tamara Pizzoli
Illustrated by Elena Tommasi Ferroni

Godmothers are more
than just fairies.

Godmothers are hand holders,

and space holders,

and friends.

Godmothers are timekeepers,

and time sharers.

Godmothers are flights of fancy.

Godmothers are promises kept,

and wept tears swept.

Godmothers are
wish makers and givers.

Godmothers are
memory makers,
and memory savers.

Godmothers are gifts.

They are lifelong gifts of love...

just for you.

www.ingramcontent.com/pod-product-compliance
Lightning Source LLC
Chambersburg PA
CBHW042008100426
42738CB00040B/107